# The International Critical Thinking Reading and Writing Test

*How to Assess Close Reading and Substantive Writing*

SECOND EDITION

RICHARD PAUL and LINDA ELDER

ROWMAN & LITTLEFIELD
*Lanham • Boulder • New York • London*

Originally published by
The Foundation for Critical Thinking
1-800-833-3645
www.criticalthinking.org

Reissued in 2019 by Rowman & Littlefield
An imprint of The Rowman & Littlefield Publishing Group, Inc.
4501 Forbes Boulevard, Suite 200, Lanham, Maryland 20706
www.rowman.com

6 Tinworth Street, London SE11 5AL, United Kingdom


Paperback edition published 2019



British Library Cataloguing in Publication Information Available

**Library of Congress Cataloging-in-Publication Data Is Available**

ISBN 978-0-944583-32-6 (pbk: alk. paper)
ISBN 978-1-5381-3396-5 (electronic)

∞™ The paper used in this publication meets the minimum requirements of American National Standard for Information Sciences—Permanence of Paper for Printed Library Materials, ANSI/NISO Z39.48-1992.

# The Foundation for Critical Thinking and the Thinker's Guide Library

Founded by Dr. Richard Paul, the Foundation for Critical Thinking is the longest-running non-profit organization dedicated to critical thinking. Through seminars and conferences, online courses and resources, and a wide range of publications, the Foundation promotes critical societies by cultivating essential intellectual abilities and virtues in every field of study and professional area. Learn more at www.criticalthinking.org and visit the Center for Critical Thinking Community Online (criticalthinking-community.org).

The Thinker's Guide Library introduces the Paul-Elder Framework for Critical Thinking™ and contextualizes critical thinking across subject areas and audience levels to foster fairminded critical reasoning throughout the world.

1. The Miniature Guide to Critical Thinking Concepts & Tools, Eighth Edition
2. The Thinker's Guide to Analytic Thinking
3. The Thinker's Guide to Ethical Reasoning
4. The Thinker's Guide to Socratic Questioning
5. The Thinker's Guide to Fallacies
6. The Nature and Functions of Critical & Creative Thinking
7. The Art of Asking Essential Questions, Fifth Edition
8. The Thinker's Guide to the Human Mind
9. The Thinker's Guide for Conscientious Citizens on How to Detect Media Bias and Propaganda in National and World News, Fourth Edition
10. The Thinker's Guide to Scientific Thinking
11. The Thinker's Guide to Engineering Reasoning
12. The Thinker's Guide to Clinical Reasoning
13. The Aspiring Thinker's Guide to Critical Thinking
14. The Student Guide to Historical Thinking
15. The Thinker's Guide for Students on How to Study & Learn a Discipline, Second Edition
16. How to Read a Paragraph: The Art of Close Reading, Second Edition
17. How to Write a Paragraph: The Art of Substantive Writing
18. The International Critical Thinking Reading and Writing Test, Second Edition
19. The Miniature Guide to Practical Ways for Promoting Active and Cooperative Learning, Third Edition
20. How to Improve Student Learning: 30 Practical Ideas
21. A Critical Thinker's Guide to Educational Fads
22. The Thinker's Guide to Intellectual Standards
23. A Guide for Educators to Critical Thinking Competency Standards

# Contents

## Introduction

Reading, Writing and the Educated Mind ....3
The Relationship Between Reading and Writing ....4
Purpose of the Test ....5
Intellectual Skills Essential to Close Reading ....5
Intellectual Skills Essential to Substantive Writing ....6
Five Levels of Close Reading and Substantive Writing ....7
The Test Format ....11
Specimen Answers ....11
Creating Your Own Prompts ....11
Grading Rubrics ....11
Choose Holistic or Individual Answer Scoring ....12
Scoring the Examination to Achieve Reliability ....12
Consequential Validity ....13
Using the Test in Pre- or Post-Instruction (or both) ....13

## Test Forms

Form AA: Paraphrasing Substantive Quotes ....14

*The Declaration of Independence*

Form A: Paraphrasing a Text Sentence by Sentence .... 15
Form B: Explicating the Thesis of a Text .... 17
Form C: Explicating the Logic of a Text .... 18
Form D: Evaluating the Logic of a Text .... 19
Form E: Role-Playing the Author .... 20

*On Civil Disobedience*

Form A: Paraphrasing a Text Sentence by Sentence .... 21
Form B: Explicating the Thesis of a Text .... 23
Form C: Explicating the Logic of a Text .... 24
Form D: Evaluating the Logic of a Text .... 25
Form E: Role-Playing the Author .... 26

*The Art of Loving*

Form A: Paraphrasing a Text Sentence by Sentence .... 27
Form B: Explicating the Thesis of a Text .... 30
Form C: Explicating the Logic of a Text .... 31
Form D: Evaluating the Logic of a Text .... 32
Form E: Role-Playing the Author .... 32

Form CC: Explicating the Logic of a Subject or Discipline .... 34

## Specimen Answers


Form AA: Paraphrasing Substantive Quotes.......... 36

*The Declaration of Independence*

Form A: Paraphrasing a Text Sentence by Sentence .......... 38

Form B: Explicating the Thesis of a Text.......... 40

Form C: Explicating the Logic of a Text .......... 41

Form D: Evaluating the Logic of a Text.......... 42

*On Civil Disobedience*

Form A: Paraphrasing a Text Sentence by Sentence .......... 43

Form B: Explicating the Thesis of a Text.......... 45

Form C: Explicating the Logic of a Text .......... 47

Form D: Evaluating the Logic of a Text.......... 50

*The Art of Loving*

Form A: Paraphrasing a Text Sentence by Sentence .......... 52

Form B: Explicating the Thesis of a Text.......... 54

Form C: Explicating the Logic of a Text .......... 55

Form D: Evaluating the Logic of a Text.......... 57

Form CC: Explicating the Logic of a Subject or Discipline as Detailed in a Textbook

The Logic of Ecology .......... 59

The Logic of Economics .......... 61


## Appendix


A: Analyzing the Logic of an Excerpt, Article, Essay, or Chapter .......... 63

# The International Critical Thinking Reading & Writing Test

## Introduction

*The International Critical Thinking Reading & Writing Test* assesses the ability of students to use reading and writing as tools for acquiring knowledge. To appreciate the significance of this test, it is important to understand the integral relationship between reading, writing, and learning.

## Reading, Writing and the Educated Mind

Educated persons routinely read closely and write substantively–to learn new ideas, to deepen their understanding of ideas, and to correct conceptual misunderstandings.

To read closely is to construct accurately the meaning of the texts one reads. It involves constructing the thinking of an author in one's own mind, in such a way that were the author to hear the summary, he or she would say, "Excellent, you understand exactly what I was saying!"

Educated persons realize that many of the most important ideas and insights are to be found only in written publications. They also realize that there is a significant difference between reading closely (and hence being able to say accurately and precisely what is said in a text) and reading superficially (and hence being able merely to express a vague, and often erroneous, facsimile of what is said in a text).

To write substantively is to say something worth saying about something worth saying something about. It involves the ability to identify important ideas and express significant implications of those ideas in clear and precise writing.

Educated persons understand the important difference between writing that is merely fluent (but says nothing worth saying) and writing that is substantial (that says something important). They realize, in other words, the difference between "style" and "substance."

To read and write with skill and insight:

1. Students need to understand *how* to read and write well. In other words, they need to understand the *theory* behind close reading and substantive writing. They need to make intuitive in their thinking the conceptual connections behind skilled reading and writing, and then to grasp how skilled reading and writing interrelate.
2. They need practice in close reading and substantive writing. If they are ever to become skilled at reading and writing, students need daily practice, over many years, in disciplined reading and writing. They must develop the habit of reading and writing for deep learning. Through this practice, they come to *learn how to learn.* They gain skills that enable them to continue learning throughout a lifetime.

## The Relationship Between Reading and Writing

There is an intimate relationship between reading well and writing well. Any significant deficiency in reading entails a parallel deficiency in writing. Any significant deficiency in writing entails a parallel deficiency in reading.

For example, if students cannot distinguish writing that is clear from writing that is unclear, there will be problems in their reading. They will, for example, mistake vague ideas for clear ones. They will think they understand when they don't. For example, suppose students read the sentence, "Democracy is a form of government in which the people rule." Students skilled in close reading will recognize that they don't really know what this sentence means until they answer the following questions: "Who exactly are *the people*?" and "What exactly is meant by the word *rule*?" In other words, they will recognize the importance of explicating the meaning of the words *people* and *rule*. They will see that understanding these concepts is essential to giving meaning to the sentence.

Similarly, if students cannot detect significant vagueness and ambiguity within texts they read, they will have difficulty formulating significant concepts as they write. In fact, to write substantively students must be able to bring ideas from a text into their thinking, arranging those ideas logically in clear prose style.

In superficial uncritical reading, students soon forget and often distort what they read. In superficial uncritical writing, students often misrepresent what is in the text. Superficial writing does not help students take ownership of the substance they write about. It produces instead an illusion of knowledge. It opens the door for multiple forms of misunderstanding.

Thus, close reading and substantive writing are symbiotic skills of disciplined thought. Both require that we think from multiple perspectives. Both require that we use the elements of reasoning well.[1] In other words, both require the intellectual ability to:

1. Clarify purposes: an author's purpose(s) (when we read), and our own purpose(s) (when we write).
2. Formulate clear questions: those that an author is asking (as we read) and those we are pursuing (as we write).
3. Distinguish accurate and relevant information from inaccurate and irrelevant information: in texts that we read and in preparation for our own writing.
4. Reach logical inferences or conclusions: based on what we read, and in preparation for writing.
5. Identify significant and deep concepts: those of an author and those we want to guide our thinking while we write.
6. Distinguish justifiable from unjustifiable assumptions: that an author is using, or that we are using in our own thinking as we write.
7. Trace logical implications: those of an author's thinking, and those that may follow from our written work.

[1] For explication of the elements of reasoning, see: Linda Elder, and Richard Paul. 2003. *A Miniature Guide to the Foundations of Analytic Thinking*. Dillon Beach, California: Foundation for Critical Thinking. www.criticalthinking.org

8. Identify and think within multiple viewpoints: those that an author presents (or fails to present when relevant) and those relevant to the issues in our written work (and that we need to include).

These are just a few examples that shed light on the intimate relationship between close reading and substantive writing and on the important connection between disciplined thought and skilled reading and writing. As students develop their abilities to read closely and write substantively, they come to see the many ways in which the two processes are related.

## Purpose of the Test

The purpose of the test is to assess students' abilities to think in particular "disciplined" and skilled ways. If used successfully, the results make it possible to determine the extent to which students have and have not learned foundational critical thinking, reading and writing skills.

## Intellectual Skills Essential to Close Reading[2]

To think within any discipline or subject, students must be able to deeply comprehend what they read. Consider the following competency standards for close reading.

### Critical Thinking Principle

Educated persons are able to read texts closely and, through that process, take ownership of the most important ideas in them. They also understand the importance of reading to learning.

### Performance Indicators and Dispositions

Students who think critically routinely read texts that are significant and thus expand their worldview. When reading, they consistently strive to accurately represent in their own thinking what they are reading in the text. Recognizing that every text has a purpose, they clarify the purpose of texts as they read them. Recognizing that close reading requires active engagement in reading, they create an inner dialog with the text as they read—questioning, summarizing and connecting important ideas with other important ideas.

### Outcomes

1. Students reflect as they read.
2. Students monitor how they are reading as they are reading—distinguishing between what they understand in the text and what they do not understand.
3. Students accurately summarize and elaborate texts (in their own words) as they read.
4. Students give examples, from their experience, of ideas in texts.
5. Students connect the core ideas in a text to other core ideas they understand.
6. Students take the core ideas they obtain through reading and apply them to their lives.
7. Students accurately paraphrase what they read (sentence by sentence).

[2] For a deeper understanding of the skills described in this competency, see: Richard Paul, and Linda Elder. 2003. *The Thinker's Guide to How to Read a Paragraph and Beyond: The Art of Close Reading.* Dillon Beach, California: Foundation for Critical Thinking. www.criticalthinking.org

8. Students accurately and logically explicate the thesis of a paragraph:
    - First, students state the main point of the paragraph in one or two sentences.
    - Second, students elaborate what they have paraphrased. ("In other words...")
    - Third, students give examples of the meaning by tying it to concrete situations in the real world. ("For example...")
    - Fourth, students generate apt illustrations: metaphors, analogies, pictures, or diagrams of the basic thesis (to connect the thesis to other meanings they already understand).
9. Students analyze the logic of what they read (its purpose, its main question, the information it contains, its main idea...)
10. Students evaluate what they read (for clarity, accuracy, precision, relevance, depth, breadth, logic, and significance, and so forth).
11. Students accurately role-play an author's viewpoint, as presented in a text.

## Intellectual Skills Essential To Substantive Writing[3]

Now consider the intellectual skills necessary to substantive writing.

### Critical Thinking Principle

Educated persons are able to write in such a way as to say something substantive. They also understand the importance of writing to learning.

### Performance Indicators and Dispositions

Students who think critically use writing as an important tool both for communicating important ideas and for learning. They use writing to deepen their understanding of important concepts and to clarify interrelationships between concepts. They consistently write in such a way as to become more clear, precise, accurate, relevant, deep, broad, logical and significant as thinkers. In writing, they are able to clearly and accurately analyze and evaluate ideas in texts and in their own thinking. They consistently learn to write as they write to learn. In other words, they use writing as an important tool for learning ideas deeply and permanently.

### Outcomes

1. Students reflect as they write.
2. Students monitor how they are writing as they are writing—distinguishing between what they understand in the text and what they do not understand.
3. Students accurately summarize (in their own words) texts they read, or ideas they hear.
4. Students routinely give examples from their experience as they write to (exemplify important ideas).
5. Students explicitly connect core ideas to other core ideas as they write.

[3] For a deeper understanding of the skills described in this competency, see: Richard Paul, and Linda Elder. 2003. *The Thinker's Guide to How to Write a Paragraph: The Art of Substantive Writing.* Dillon Beach, California: Foundation for Critical Thinking. www.criticalthinking.org

6. Students write about ideas that apply to their lives.
7. Students demonstrate the ability to explicate in writing the thesis they are developing or defending.
    - They state their main point.
    - They elaborate their main point.
    - They give examples of what they mean.
    - They create analogies and metaphors that help readers understand what they mean.
8. Students demonstrate the ability to clearly and accurately analyze, in writing, the logic of a text, chapter, academic subject, significant concept, and so on: (its purpose, its main question, the information it contains, its main idea…)
9. Students consistently use universal intellectual standards in their writing, routinely checking their writing for clarity, accuracy, precision, relevance, depth, breadth, logic, significance, and fairness and so forth.

## Five Levels of Close Reading and Substantive Writing

There are at least five levels of close reading and substantive writing. Our purpose in this test is to determine the test-taker's ability to read and write at one or more of these five levels of proficiency.

### First Level—Paraphrasing

The first level of reading proficiency is that of accurately translating an author's wording into our own. In other words, we put the words and thoughts of the author into our words. Our paraphrase is successful only to the extent that our words capture the essential meaning of the original text, only to the extent that it makes intelligible the meaning of the original text.

Hence, if we read the following in a text: "democracy is rule by the people," our paraphrase of it might read, "Democracy exists only to the extent that there is a broad basis of equality of political power among the people at large. This means that all people within the state should have relatively equal power and equal input in determining what the laws will be. By implication, a state fails to be democratic to the extent that a few people—whether they be wealthy or otherwise influential—have significantly more political power than others." The paraphrase helps open up the text because it points us to possible problems in assessing the degree to which any country is democratic—for example, "Does it restrict the influence of the wealthy so they cannot use it to exercise a disproportionate influence in the decision-making of the government?"

### Second Level—Explicating

In this proficiency we assess the thinker's (reader's) ability to state, elaborate, exemplify, and illustrate the thesis of a paragraph. Consider the four questions that can be used to assess writing for clarity:

1. Could you state your basic point in one simple sentence?

2. Could you elaborate your basic point more fully (in other words)?
3. Could you give an example of your point?
4. Could you give an analogy or metaphor to help clarify what you mean?

Each of these clarification strategies requires substantive writing skills.

**Clarification Strategies**

- **The ability to state a thesis clearly in a sentence.** If we cannot accurately state our key idea in a sentence using our own words, we don't really know what we want to say.
- **The ability to explain a thesis sentence in greater detail.** If we cannot elaborate our key idea, then we have not yet connected its meaning to other concepts we understand.
- **The ability to give examples of what we are saying.** If we cannot connect what we have elaborated with concrete situations in the real world, our understanding of the meanings is still abstract, and, to some extent, vague.
- **The ability to illustrate what we are saying with a metaphor, analogy, picture, diagram, or drawing.** If we cannot generate metaphors, analogies, pictures, or diagrams of the meanings we are constructing, we have not yet connected what we understand with other domains of knowledge and experience.

## Third Level—Analysis

At this level of proficiency we assess the student's ability to identify the following:

- The author's *purpose* in writing the text.
- The most important *question,* problem, or issue in the text.
- The most significant *information* or data in the text.
- The most basic *conclusion* in the text.
- The most basic *concepts,* theories, or ideas in the text.
- The most fundamental *assumptions* of the text.
- The most significant *implications* of the text.
- The *point of view* in the text.

## Fourth Level—Evaluation

In this level of proficiency we assess the student's ability to evaluate or assess the text using eight basic intellectual standards.

## Fifth Level—Role-Playing

In this level of proficiency, we assess the student's ability to actively role-play the thinking of the author.

These levels are summarized in the following chart, and written as directions for students.

## First Level: Paraphrasing

### Paraphrasing the Text Sentence by Sentence

1. State in your own words the meaning of each sentence as you read.

## Second Level: Explicating

### Explicating the Thesis of a Paragraph

1. State the main point of the paragraph in one or two sentences.
2. Then elaborate on what you have paraphrased ("In other words,…").
3. Give examples of the meaning by tying it to concrete situations in the real world. (For example,…)
4. Generate metaphors, analogies, pictures, or diagrams of the basic thesis to connect it to other meanings you already understand.

## Third Level: Analysis

### Analyzing the Logic of Text

Anytime you read, you are reading the product of an author's reasoning. You can use your understanding of the elements of reasoning, therefore, to bring your reading to a higher level. You can do this by writing your answers to the following questions (you may ask these questions in any order you want):

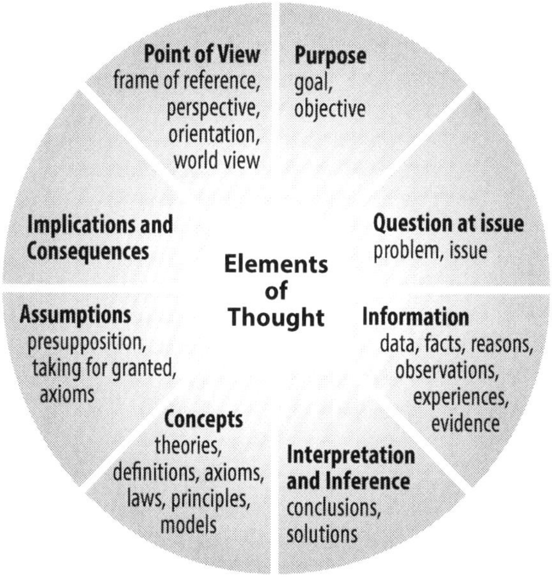


Use the template in Appendix A, *Analyzing the Logic of an Excerpt, Article, Essay, or Chapter,*

## Fourth Level: Evaluation

### Assessing the Logic of What We Are Reading

Every written piece is not of the same quality. You assess what you read by applying intellectual standards to it, standards such as *clarity, precision, accuracy, relevance, significance, depth, breadth, logic,* and *fairness*. Some authors adhere to some standards while violating others. For example, an author might be *clear* in stating his or her position, while at the same time using information that is not *accurate*. An author might use *relevant* information but fail to think through the complexities of the issue (that is, fail to achieve *depth*). An author's argument might be *logical* but not *significant*. As a reader, then, you need to become adept at assessing the quality of an author's reasoning. You do this *only when* you can accurately state in your own words an author's meaning.

To assess an author's work, answer the following questions:

- Does the author *clearly* state his or her meaning, or is the text vague, confused, or muddled in some way?
- Is the author *accurate* in what he or she claims?
- Is the author sufficiently *precise* in providing details and specifics when specifics are relevant?
- Does the author introduce *irrelevant* material, thereby wandering from his/her purpose?
- Does the author take us into the important *complexities* inherent in the subject, or is the writing *superficial*?
- Does the author consider other *relevant* points of view, or is the writing overly *narrow* in its perspective?
- Is the text internally *consistent,* or does the text contain unexplained contradictions?
- Is the text *significant,* or is the subject dealt with in a trivial manner?
- Does the author display *fairness,* or does the author take a one-sided, narrow approach?

## Fifth Level: Role-Playing

### Speaking In the Voice of an Author

Role-playing an author is, in one way, the ultimate test of understanding. When you role-play, in essence you say: "Look, I will enter the mind of the author and speak as if I were the author. I will discuss any questions you may have about the text by adopting the voice of the author and will answer your questions as I think the author would. I will speak in the first person singular. I will be like an actor playing the part of Hamlet. I will try to be the author fully and truly for the purpose of this exercise."

To role-play an author, you need a partner who has read the text and is willing to ask you important questions about it. Responding to questions forces you to think within the author's logic. Practicing talking within the voice of an author is a good way to get a personal sense of whether you have really absorbed the core meanings of a text.

If you are working alone, write out a dialogue between the author and a questioner attempting to understand the logic of the author's reasoning.

## The Test Format

There are five primary student forms in the test that link together (Forms A-E). The entire test (every form) need not be included in any given testing situation. For example, you may decide to use the forms that focus on the first and second levels of close reading and substantive writing at one time, and the third, fourth, and fifth levels later. Many different combinations of the forms might be used for a given testing situation.

In addition to the four primary test forms, there are two additional forms—Form AA, which focuses on paraphrasing short quotes, and Form CC, which focuses on formulating the logic of a subject or discipline. Forms AA and CC are logically parallel to forms A and C respectively.

## Specimen Answers

For four of the five primary forms (A–D), we provide 12 specimen answers (three for each form). We also provide examples of answers for forms AA, and CC. We suggest that test graders complete each test form themselves before reading our specimen answers. View our answers not as the right answers, but simply reasonable answers. It is important that both teachers and students understand that there are multiple ways to accurately paraphrase a text, to explicate the thesis of a text, to explicate the reasoning embedded in a text. What you will be assessing in student work is their ability to capture the essence of a sentence, phrase, or text, the essence of the author's reasoning, and so forth.

Students should be provided with a dictionary or thesaurus and instructed to look up any words when they are unsure how to express a given word or phrase in their own words. They should be instructed not to rush the test; and they should be allowed ample time to work through the complexities of each form of the test at their own pace. They should be encouraged to work at each sentence until they are satisfied that they have captured the essential meaning of it as precisely as they can. We want students to understand that critical reading and writing take time and perseverance. It is far better to assign only a few forms, with ample time for students to competently complete their work, than to assign more forms than students can reasonably work through in a given test situation.

## Creating Your Own Prompts

As you read through the test forms, you will see that they can be used with an unlimited number of excerpts and subjects. Should you decide to use your own texts you will need to create sample answers. The main point is that the format used throughout the test can be used again and again, using different text prompts within any discipline or subject.

## Grading Rubrics

For each test form, test graders will use a 1–10 point scoring scale. The following guidelines outline how student answers should be graded. The total points possible will depend on whether one grades each item within every test form or grades each form holistically.

**Points Guideline**

0–2 points—unacceptable (unskilled). The answer is inaccurate and/or unclear.

3–4 points—poor (minimally skilled). The answer, though partially accurate and minimally clear, is significantly inaccurate or misleading.

5–6 points—mixed level (beginning skills). The answer is clear but not perfectly accurate. It is partially correct and partially incorrect.

7–8 points—commendable (skilled). The answer is well expressed, though with minor problems. It is basically correct and clear. Any misunderstanding is minor.

9–10 points—excellent (highly skilled). The answer is accurate, insightful, clearly and precisely stated, and well exemplified (when an example is relevant).

## Choose Holistic or Individual Answer Scoring

The grading rubrics can be used for each individual answer within a form or holistically for the entire form. If a score is given for each part within a form, after scoring is completed individual scores will then need to be averaged to obtain an overall score for that form. For example, for Form AA—Paraphrasing Substantive Quotes, if the text being paraphrased is divided into eight sections, graders might score each of the eight sections according to its clarity and accuracy (as outlined in the grading rubrics). Once answers for all eight sections have been individually scored, points for each section would be added and then divided by eight to get the average score for the entire form.

In order to achieve accuracy in grading, we suggest that this individual scoring format be used before holistic scoring is attempted.

To test the accuracy of holistic grading, graders should use the following procedure:

1. Begin by giving a holistic score to answers within a form, then
2. score answers for each section within the form, then
3. average scores for answers given for individual answers, then
4. compare this average score with the holistic score given initially.

Once graders can ensure that holistic scores for answers on the entire form match average scores for section scoring, they can move to holistic grading as a rule.

## Scoring the Examination to Achieve Reliability

Before grading the test, graders should review the basic theory of critical thinking, close reading, and substantive writing.[4] To ensure that student answers are not misgraded, only those with a basic understanding of critical thinking should grade test papers. To achieve reliability in grading, the following guidelines should be followed:

- Prior to grading the test, graders should also "take the test" themselves, and then compare their answers to our specimen answers.

[4] We recommend the following background reading material: *The Thinker's Guide to Analytic Thinking; The Thinker's Guide to how to Read a Paragraph; The Thinker's Guide to How to Write a Paragraph; Critical Thinking: Learn the Tools the Best Thinkers Use* (chapters 2–3). These publications can be found at www.criticalthinking.org.

- Test graders should reach consensus on the range of plausible interpretations for any particular test form.
- Once a consensus is achieved, all participating graders should assess several forms completed by students and then compare scoring results by each grader.
- The result should be within a one-point range. That is, the margin of error for graders should be plus or minus one point. Graders should work with at least two other faculty graders until the scoring of the exams falls consistently within this range.

**Applying the Grading Rubrics to Our Specimen Answers**

We consider each of specimen answers to be at the level of *excellent*, though some might benefit from further elaboration.

## Consequential Validity

This test, when used appropriately and graded accurately, should lead to a high degree of *consequential validity*. In other words, the use of the test should cause teachers to teach in such a way as to foster close reading and substantive writing abilities. For example, for students to perform well on Form AA, they must be able to accurately paraphrase what they read. They will not be able to effectively do this if they have not been taught the skills necessary for doing so. They will need practice in it. Therefore, teachers will need to design instruction so that students learn how to accurately paraphrase, and get adequate practice in paraphrasing. Similarly, for students to perform well on Forms A and B, teachers will need to design instruction so that students get routine practice in stating, elaborating, exemplifying, and illustrating the thesis of a text. In addition, for students to perform well on Forms C and D, teachers will need to teach students how to analyze and assess reasoning and give them practice in doing so.

In other words, for students to perform well on the test, teachers will need to design instruction so that students *can* perform well on the test. Students cannot become skilled in paraphrasing without practice in it. Students cannot become skilled in summarizing a thesis without practice in it. They cannot become skilled in analyzing and assessing reasoning without practice in it. However, when they have routine practice in paraphrasing, summarizing, analyzing, and assessing, they will develop skills of mind requisite to learning well within any subject or discipline, and thinking well within any domain of human life.

In short, use of the test should lead students to learn some of the most important skills they need to function in the world as educated persons.

## Using the Test in Pre- or Post-Instruction (or both)

Any part of the test can be used in pre- or post-instruction format in order to assess improvement in skills after instruction and/or to gather data for research purposes.

# The International Critical Thinking Reading and Writing Test Form AA

## Paraphrasing Substantive Quotes

**Directions:** For each of the quotes in this section, paraphrase in your own words the meaning of the quote.

He who passively accepts evil is as much involved in it as he who helps to perpetuate it.

*—Martin Luther King, Jr.*

Every effort to confine Americanism to a single pattern, to constrain it to a single formula, is disloyalty to everything that is valid in Americanism.

*—Henry Steele Commager*

In a free society, standards of public morality can be measured only by whether physical coercion—violence against persons or property—occurs. There is no right to be offended by words, actions, or symbols.

*—Richard E. Sincere, Jr.*

Liberty is the only thing you cannot have unless you are willing to give it to others.

*—William Allen White*

I can't understand why people are frightened of new ideas. I'm frightened of the old ones.

*—John Cage*

The legitimate powers of government extend to such acts as are only injurious to others.

*—Thomas Jefferson*

The propagandist's purpose is to make one set of people forget that certain other sets of people are human.

*—Aldous Huxley*

The shepherd always tries to persuade the sheep that their interests and his own are the same.

*—Stendhal*

# The Declaration of Independence
# Form A

## Paraphrasing A Text Sentence by Sentence

**Background Understandings:** From the Declaration of Independence, July 4, 1776.

To make sense of this paragraph one must understand that it is part of a political manifesto adopted by the Continental Congress proclaiming the independence of the thirteen British colonies in America from Great Britain.

When in the Course of human events, it becomes necessary for one people to dissolve the political bands which have connected them with another, and to assume among the powers of the earth, the separate and equal station to which the Laws of Nature and of Nature's God entitle them, a decent respect to the opinions of mankind requires that they should declare the causes which impel them to the separation.

We hold these truths to be self-evident, that all men are created equal, that they are endowed by their Creator with certain unalienable Rights, that among these are Life, Liberty and the pursuit of happiness. That to secure these rights, Governments are instituted among Men, deriving their just powers from the consent of the governed, That whenever any Form of Government becomes destructive of these ends, it is the Right of the People to alter or abolish it, and to institute new Government, laying its foundation on such principles and organizing its powers in such form, as to them shall seem most likely to effect their Safety and Happiness. Prudence, indeed, will dictate that Governments long established should not be changed for light and transient causes; and accordingly all experience hath shown that mankind are more disposed to suffer, while evils are sufferable, than to right themselves by abolishing the forms to which they are accustomed. But when a long train of abuses and usurpations, pursuing invariably the same Object evinces a design to reduce them under absolute Despotism, it is their right, it is their duty, to throw off such Government, and to provide new Guards for their future security.

**Directions:** Paraphrase the text above in sections, as indicated below.

*When in the course of human events, it becomes necessary for one people to dissolve the political bands which have connected them with another,*

PARAPHRASE:

---

*and to assume among the powers of the earth, the separate and equal station to which the Laws of Nature and of Nature's God entitle them,*

PARAPHRASE:

*a decent respect to the opinions of mankind requires that they should declare the causes which impel them to the separation.*

PARAPHRASE:

---

*We hold these truths to be self-evident, that all men are created equal, that they are endowed by their Creator with certain unalienable Rights, that among these are Life, Liberty and the pursuit of happiness.*

PARAPHRASE:

---

*That to secure these rights, Governments are instituted among Men, deriving their just powers from the consent of the governed,*

PARAPHRASE:

---

*That whenever any Form of Government becomes destructive of these ends, it is the Right of the People to alter or abolish it,*

PARAPHRASE:

---

*and to institute new Government, laying its foundation on such principles and organizing its powers in such form, as to them shall seem most likely to effect their Safety and Happiness.*

PARAPHRASE:

---

*Prudence, indeed, will dictate that Governments long established should not be changed for light and transient causes;*

PARAPHRASE:

---

*and accordingly all experience hath shown that mankind are more disposed to suffer, while evils are sufferable, than to right themselves by abolishing the forms to which they are accustomed.*

PARAPHRASE:

---

*But when a long train of abuses and usurpations, pursuing invariably the same Object evinces a design to reduce them under absolute Despotism, it is their right, it is their duty, to throw off such Government, and to provide new Guards for their future security.*

PARAPHRASE:

# The Declaration of Independence
# Form B

## Explicating the Thesis of a Text

**Directions:** After reading the excerpt from the Declaration of Independence, complete the following four tasks:

1. State the thesis of the passage in your own words.
2. Elaborate the thesis with additional explanation. ("In other words…")
3. Give one or more examples of the thesis.
4. Illustrate the thesis with a metaphor or analogy.

# The Declaration of Independence
# Form C

## Explicating the Logic of a Text
### (An analysis of eight basic structures)

**Directions:** After reading the Declaration of Independence, express clearly and precisely:

1. The author's *purpose*.
2. The most important *question,* problem, or issue in the excerpt.
3. The most significant *information* or data in the excerpt.
4. The most basic *conclusion* in the excerpt.
5. The most basic *concepts,* theories, or ideas in the excerpt.
6. The most fundamental *assumptions* of the excerpt.
7. The most significant *implications* of the excerpt.
8. The *point of view* in the excerpt.

See Appendix A: The Logic of an Excerpt, Article, Essay, or Chapter for a full template.

# The Declaration of Independence
# Form D

## Evaluating the Logic of a Text

**Directions:** Assess the text according to eight basic intellectual standards.

1. Does the author express what he/she means clearly (or is the text vague, confused, or muddled in some way)?
2. Is the author accurate in what he/she claims?
3. Is the author sufficiently precise (providing details and specifics when they are relevant)?
4. Does the author wander from his/her purpose (thereby introducing irrelevant material)?
5. Does the author take us into the important complexities inherent in the subject (or is the writing superficial)?
6. Does the author consider other relevant points of view (or is the writing overly narrow in its perspective)?
7. Is the text internally consistent (or are there contradictions in the text)?
8. Is what the text says significant (or is the subject dealt with in a trivial manner)? Does the author display fairness (or is the subject dealt with in an unfair manner)?

# The Declaration of Independence
# Form E

## Role-Playing the Author

**Directions:** Role-play the principal author of the declaration, Thomas Jefferson, by constructing a dialogue between him and an intelligent questioner who asks him to explain various portions of the text

Respond to the questions as if you were Jefferson. Have the questioner ask whatever questions you would imagine might occur to such a person about what the declaration means. Answer by trying to reconstruct what you think Jefferson might say. Make sure that what you "attribute" to him is implied in some way in the text. We have begun the dialogue for you. Your job is to continue it.

**Questioner:** Mr. Jefferson, why did you write this document?

Jefferson: I wrote this document to justify the American colonies in separating themselves politically from Great Britain. I believe that all people on earth have the right, the basic human right, to freely choose the way they are governed.

**Questioner:** Under what conditions do you think that people are justified in attempting to overthrow their government?

Jefferson:

Questioner:

Jefferson:

*Continue dialog…*

# On Civil Disobedience
# Form A
## Paraphrasing A Text Sentence by Sentence

**Background Understandings.** From an essay on civil disobedience (pp. 635, 636–637, 644), originally written in 1849 by Henry David Thoreau,[5] a well-known scholar in 19th Century American cultural and literary thought.

I heartily accept the motto, "That government is best which governs least"; and I should like to see it acted up to more rapidly and systematically. Carried out, it finally amounts to this, which also I believe, "That government is best which governs not at all"; and when men are prepared for it, that will be the kind of government which they will have. Government is at best but an expedient; but most governments are usually, and all governments are sometimes, inexpedient. The objections which have been brought against a standing army, and they are many and weighty, and deserve to prevail, may also at last be brought against a standing government. The standing army is only an arm of the standing government. The government itself, which is only the mode which the people have chosen to execute their will, is equally liable to be abused and perverted before the people can act through it.

Can there not be a government in which majorities do not virtually decide right and wrong, but conscience?...Must the citizen ever for a moment, or in the least degree, resign his conscience, to the legislator? Why has every man a conscience then? I think that we should be men first, and subjects afterward. It is not desirable to cultivate a respect for the law, so much as for the right. The only obligation which I have a right to assume is to do at any time what I think right....If the injustice is part of the necessary friction of the machine of government, let it go, let it go;...If the injustice has a spring, or a pulley, or a rope, or a crank, exclusively for itself, then perhaps you can consider whether the remedy will not be worse than the evil; but if it is of such a nature that it requires you to be the agent of injustice to another, then, I say, break the law. Let your life be a counter friction to stop the machine.

**Directions:** Paraphrase the text above in sections, as indicated below.

*I heartily accept the motto, "That government is best which governs least"; and I should like to see it acted up to more rapidly and systematically.*

PARAPHRASE:

---

*Carried out, it finally amounts to this, which also I believe, "That government is best that governs not at all";*

PARAPHRASE:

---

[5] Thoreau, Henry David. 1937. *Walden and Other Writings.* New York: The Modern Library.

*and when men are prepared for it, that will be the kind of government which they will have.*

PARAPHRASE:

---

*Government is at best but an expedient; but most governments are usually, and all governments are sometimes, inexpedient.*

PARAPHRASE:

---

*The objections which have been brought against a standing army, and they are many and weighty, and deserve to prevail, may also at last be brought against a standing government. The standing army is only an arm of the standing government. The government itself, which is only the mode which the people have chosen to execute their will, is equally liable to be abused and perverted before the people can act through it.*

PARAPHRASE:

---

*Can there not be a government in which majorities do not virtually decide right and wrong, but conscience?*

PARAPHRASE:

---

*Must the citizen ever for a moment, or in the least degree, resign his conscience, to the legislator? Why has every man a conscience then? I think that we should be men first, and subjects afterward.*

PARAPHRASE:

---

*It is not desirable to cultivate a respect for the law, so much as for the right. The only obligation which I have a right to assume is to do at any time what I think right.*

PARAPHRASE:

---

*If the injustice is part of the necessary friction of the machine of government, let it go, let it go;...If the injustice has a spring, or a pulley, or a rope, or a crank, exclusively for itself, then perhaps you can consider whether the remedy will not be worse than the evil;*

PARAPHRASE:

---

*but if it is of such a nature that it requires you to be the agent of injustice to another, then, I say, break the law. Let your life be a counter friction to stop the machine.*

PARAPHRASE:

# *On Civil Disobedience*
# Form B
## Explicating the Thesis of a Text

**Directions:** After reading the excerpt from *On Civil Disobedience,* complete the following four tasks:

1. State the thesis of the passage in your own words.
2. Elaborate the thesis with additional explanation. ("In other words…")
3. Give one or more examples of the thesis.
4. Illustrate the thesis with a metaphor or analogy.

# *On Civil Disobedience*
# Form C

## Explicating the Logic of a Text
### (An analysis of eight basic structures)

**Directions:** After reading the excerpt from *On Civil Disobedience,* express clearly and precisely:

1. The author's *purpose.*
2. The most important *question,* problem, or issue in the excerpt.
3. The most significant *information* or data in the excerpt.
4. The most basic *conclusion* in the excerpt.
5. The most basic *concepts,* theories, or ideas in the excerpt.
6. The most fundamental *assumptions* of excerpt.
7. The most significant *implications* of the excerpt.
8. The *point of view* in the excerpt.

See Appendix A: The Logic of an Excerpt, Article, Essay, or Chapter for a full template.

# *On Civil Disobedience*
# Form D

## Evaluating the Logic of a Text

**Directions:** Assess the text according to eight basic intellectual standards.

1. Does the author express what the he/she means **clearly** (or is the text vague, confused, or muddled in some way)?
2. Is the author **accurate** in what he/she claims?
3. Is the author sufficiently **precise** (providing details and specifics when they are relevant)?
4. Does the author wander from his/her purpose (thereby introducing **irrelevant** material)?
5. Does the author take us into the important complexities inherent in the subject (or is the writing **superficial**)?
6. Does the author consider other relevant points of view (or is the writing overly **narrow** in its perspective)?
7. Is the text internally consistent (or are there **contradictions** in the text)?
8. Is what the text says **significant** (or is the subject dealt with in a trivial manner)? Does the author display **fairness** (or is the subject dealt with in an unfair manner)?

# *On Civil Disobedience*
# Form E
## Role-Playing the Author

**Directions:** Role-play the author of the text, Henry David Thoreau, by constructing a dialogue between him and an intelligent questioner who asks him to explain various portions of the text.

Respond to the questions as if you were Thoreau. Have the questioner ask whatever questions you would imagine might occur to such a person about what the text means. Answer by trying to reconstruct what you think Thoreau might say. Make sure that what you "attribute" to him is implied in some way in the text. We have begun the dialogue for you. Your job is to continue it.

**Questioner:** Tell me why you wrote this text. What was your purpose?

Thoreau: My purpose was to convince people that governments are often, if not usually, corrupt. In other words, governments tend to serve themselves, rather that the people to whom they owe allegiance.

Questioner: What is it that you think people should do, with respect to their government?

Thoreau: First and foremost, people need to be true to their own beliefs and stand up for those believes, even if it means going against the government.

Questioner:

Thoreau:

Questioner:

*Continue dialog…*

# *The Art of Loving*
# Form A

## Paraphrasing A Text Sentence by Sentence

**Background Understandings.** From the book, *The Art of Loving* (pp. 1–2, 23–24, 47), written in1956, by the distinguished psychologist, Erich Fromm.[6]

Is love an art? Then it requires knowledge and effort. Or is love a pleasant sensation, which to experience is a matter of chance, something one "falls into" if one is lucky? This little book is based on the former premise, while undoubtedly the majority of people today believe in the latter.

Not that people think that love is not important. They are starved for it; they watch endless numbers of films about happy and unhappy love stories, they listen to hundreds of trashy songs about love—yet hardly anyone thinks that there is anything that needs to be learned about love.

This peculiar attitude is based on several premises which either singly or combined tend to uphold it. Most people see the problem of love primarily as that of being loved, rather than that of loving, of one's capacity to love. Hence the problem to them is how to be loved, how to be lovable. In pursuit of this aim they follow several paths. One, which is especially used by men, is to be successful, to be as powerful and rich as the social margin of one's position permits. Another, used especially by women, is to make oneself attractive, by cultivating one's body, dress, etc. Other ways of making oneself attractive, used both by men and women, are to develop pleasant manners, interesting conversation, to be helpful, modest, inoffensive. Many of the ways to make oneself lovable are the same as those used to make oneself successful, "to win friends and influence people." As a matter of fact, what most people in our culture mean by being lovable is essentially a mixture between being popular and having sex appeal.

The active character of love becomes evident in the fact that it always implies certain basic elements, common to all forms of love. These are care, responsibility, respect, and knowledge.…Love is the active concern for the life and the growth of that which we love.…Respect is the ability to see a person as he is, to be aware of his unique individuality. Respect means the concern that the other person should grow and unfold as he is. Respect, thus, implies the absence of exploitation. I want the loved person to grow and unfold for his own sake, and in his own ways, and not for the purpose of serving me. If I love the other person, I feel one with him or her, but with him as he is, not as I need him to be as an object for my use. It is clear that respect is possible only if I have achieved independence; if I can stand and walk without needing crutches, without having to dominate and exploit anyone else. Respect exists only on the basis of freedom: "l'amour est l'enfant de la liberté" as an old French song says; love is the child of freedom, never of domination.…To love somebody is not just a strong feeling—it is a decision, it is a judgment, it is a promise.

---

6 Fromm, Erich. 1956. *The Art of Loving*. New York: Harper and Row.

**Directions:** Paraphrase the text from the previous page in sections, as indicated below.

*Is love an art? Then it requires knowledge and effort.*

PARAPHRASE:

*Or is love a pleasant sensation, which to experience is a matter of chance, something one "falls into" if one is lucky?*

PARAPHRASE:

*This little book is based on the former premise, while undoubtedly the majority of people today believe in the latter.*

PARAPHRASE:

*Not that people think that love is not important. They are starved for it; they watch endless numbers of films about happy and unhappy love stories, they listen to hundreds of trashy songs about love—yet hardly anyone thinks that there is anything that needs to be learned about love.*

PARAPHRASE:

*This peculiar attitude is based on several premises which either singly or combined tend to uphold it. Most people see the problem of love primarily as that of being loved, rather than that of loving, of one's capacity to love. Hence the problem to them is how to be loved, how to be lovable.*

PARAPHRASE:

*In pursuit of this aim they follow several paths. One, which is especially used by men, is to be successful, to be as powerful and rich as the social margin of one's position permits. Another, used especially by women, is to make oneself attractive, by cultivating one's body, dress, etc.*

PARAPHRASE:

*Other ways of making oneself attractive, used both by men and women, are to develop pleasant manners, interesting conversation, to be helpful, modest, inoffensive. Many of the ways to make oneself lovable are the same as those used to make oneself successful, "to win friends and influence people." As a matter of fact, what most people in our culture mean by being lovable is essentially a mixture between being popular and having sex appeal.*

PARAPHRASE:

---

*The active character of love becomes evident in the fact that it always implies certain basic elements, common to all forms of love. These are care, responsibility, respect, and knowledge....Love is the active concern for the life and the growth of that which we love....*

PARAPHRASE:

---

*Respect is the ability to see a person as he is, to be aware of his unique individuality. Respect means the concern that the other person should grow and unfold as he is. Respect, thus, implies the absence of exploitation. I want the loved person to grow and unfold for his own sake, and in his own ways, and not for the purpose of serving me. If I love the other person, I feel one with him or her, but with him as he is, not as I need him to be as an object for my use.*

PARAPHRASE:

---

*It is clear that respect is possible only if I have achieved independence; if I can stand and walk without needing crutches, without having to dominate and exploit anyone else. Respect exists only on the basis of freedom: "l'amour est l'enfant de la liberté"as an old French song says; love is the child of freedom, never of domination....*

PARAPHRASE:

---

*To love somebody is not just a strong feeling—it is a decision, it is a judgment, it is a promise.*

PARAPHRASE:

# *The Art of Loving*
# Form B

## Explicating the Thesis of a Text

**Directions:** After reading the excerpt from *The Art of Loving,* complete the following four tasks:

1. State the thesis of the passage in your own words.
2. Elaborate the thesis with additional explanation. ("In other words…")
3. Give one or more examples of the thesis.
4. Illustrate the thesis with a metaphor or analogy.

# *The Art of Loving*
# Form C

## Explicating the Logic of a Text
### (An analysis of eight basic structures)

**Directions:** After reading the excerpt from *The Art of Loving,* express clearly and precisely:

1. The author's *purpose.*
2. The most important *question,* problem, or issue in the excerpt.
3. The most significant *information* or data in the excerpt.
4. The most basic *conclusion* in the excerpt.
5. The most basic *concepts,* theories, or ideas in the excerpt.
6. The most fundamental *assumptions* of excerpt.
7. The most significant *implications* of the excerpt.
8. The *point of view* in the excerpt.

See Appendix A: The Logic of an Excerpt, Article, Essay, or Chapter for a full template.

# *The Art of Loving*
# Form D
## Evaluating the Logic of a Text

**Directions:** Assess the text according to eight basic intellectual standards.

1. Does the author express what the he/she means **clearly** (or is the text vague, confused, or muddled in some way)?
2. Is the author **accurate** in what he/she claims?
3. Is the author sufficiently **precise** (providing details and specifics when they are relevant)?
4. Does the author wander from his/her purpose (thereby introducing **irrelevant** material)?
5. Does the author take us into the important complexities inherent in the subject (or is the writing **superficial**)?
6. Does the author consider other relevant points of view (or is the writing overly **narrow** in its perspective)?
7. Is the text internally consistent (or are there **contradictions** in the text)?
8. Is what the text says **significant** (or is the subject dealt with in a trivial manner)? Does the author display **fairness** (or is the subject dealt with in an unfair manner)?

# *The Art of Loving*
# Form E
## Role-Playing the Author

**Directions:** Role-play the author of the text, Erich Fromm, by constructing a dialogue between him and an intelligent questioner who asks him to explain various portions of the text.

Respond to the questions as if you were Fromm. Have the questioner ask whatever questions you would imagine might occur to such a person about what the text means. Answer by trying to reconstruct what you think Fromm might say. Make sure that what you "attribute" to him is implied in some way in the text. We have begun the dialogue for you. Your job is to continue it.

**Questioner:** Mr. Fromm, tell me, briefly, how you think of the concept of "love."

Mr. Fromm: Well, there are different forms of love, of course, and yet there is an essence to love that one must understand if one is to be able to love, and to be loved in turn.

Questioner: So, what is the essence of love?

Mr. Fromm:

Questioner:

Mr. Fromm:

*Continue dialog...*

# Form CC

## Explicating the Logic of a Subject or Discipline as Detailed in a Textbook

When you understand and have internalized the elements of reasoning, you realize that all subjects, all disciplines, have a fundamental logic defined by the structures of thought embedded in them.

To lay bare a subject's most fundamental logic, focusing on a specific subject or discipline, answer the following questions (use textbooks, encyclopedias, and/or other relevant resources available to you):

1. What is the main *purpose* or *goal* of studying this subject? What are people in this field trying to accomplish?
2. What kinds of *questions* do they ask? What kinds of problems do they try to solve?
3. What sorts of *information* or data do they gather? How do they go about gathering information in ways that are distinctive to this field?
4. What types of *inferences* or judgments do they typically make? (Judgments about…)
5. What are the most basic ideas, *concepts* or theories in this field?
6. What do professionals in this field take for granted or *assume?*
7. What *implications* follow from studying this discipline? How are the products of this field used in everyday life?
8. How should studying this field affect my view of the world? What *viewpoint* is fostered in this field?

# The International Critical Thinking Reading and Writing Test Specimen Answers

In this section, we provide specimen answers that can be used as guides for grading student answers. For directions in how to use this section, see p. 11.

# Specimen Answers—Form AA

## Paraphrasing Substantive Quotes

*He who passively accepts evil is as much involved in it as he who helps to perpetuate it.*

—*Martin Luther King, Jr.*

PARAPHRASE: People who see unethical things being done to others but who fail to intervene (when they are able to intervene) are as unethical as those who are causing harm in the first place.

---

*Every effort to confine Americanism to a single pattern, to constrain it to a single formula, is disloyalty to everything that is valid in Americanism.*

—*Henry Steele Commager*

PARAPHRASE: There is no one "right way" to be an American. When everyone in America is expected to think within one belief system, when people are ostracized or persecuted for thinking autonomously, when people are labeled "Un-American" for independent thinking, the only legitimate definition of "true American" is annulled.

---

*In a free society, standards of public morality can be measured only by whether physical coercion—violence against persons or property—occurs. There is no right not to be offended by words, actions, or symbols.*

—*Richard E. Sincere, Jr.*

PARAPHRASE: Ethics in a free society is determined by whether violence has occurred against a person or one's property. People do not have the right to be protected against being shocked by the life-styles of others.

---

*Liberty is the only thing you cannot have unless you are willing to give it to others.*

—*William Allen White*

PARAPHRASE: If you want to be free, you have to allow others their freedom.

***I can't understand why people are frightened of new ideas. I'm frightened of the old ones.***

*—John Cage*

PARAPHRASE: Many of the ideas that have permeated human thinking throughout the years are harmful or dangerous. An old idea is not necessarily a good idea, nor is a new idea necessarily a bad one.

---

***The legitimate powers of government extend to such acts as are only injurious to others.***

*—Thomas Jefferson*

PARAPHRASE: The only authority government should have is to stop people from harming one another.

---

***The propagandist's purpose is to make one set of people forget that certain other sets of people are human.***

*—Aldous Huxley*

PARAPHRASE: The goal of propaganda is to convince people that other groups of people are inhuman, and therefore not worthy of respect and just treatment.

---

***The shepherd always tries to persuade the sheep that their interests and his own are the same.***

*—Stendhal*

PARAPHRASE: People in control always try to manipulate people into believing that what is good for those in control is good for the people as well.

# The Declaration of Independence Specimen Answers—Form A

## Paraphrasing A Text Sentence by Sentence

***When in the Course of human events, it becomes necessary for one people to dissolve the political bands which have connected them with another,***

PARAPHRASE: "Political" arrangements (forms of government) are not necessarily permanent. It is important sometimes to abolish them and set up new arrangements. When this is true, one group of people have to separate themselves from the group to which they were formerly joined.

---

***and to assume among the powers of the earth, the separate and equal station to which the laws of Nature and of Nature's God entitle them,***

PARAPHRASE: No government should dominate any other government, but all should have the same status (be "separate and equal"). The act of a people declaring themselves independent of other peoples (with whom they were formerly connected) is a perfectly natural act based on "the laws of nature." Therefore, the thirteen states are "entitled" by natural law to revolt and declare themselves "separate [from] and equal" to all other countries of the world.

---

***a decent respect to the opinions of mankind requires that they should declare the causes which impel them to the separation.***

PARAPHRASE: But when a people decide to break away from another people and establish their own nation, they should—out of respect for the views of other peoples in the world—lay out the reasons that have led them to make their revolutionary decision.

---

***We hold these truths to be self-evident, that all men are created equal, that they are endowed by their Creator with certain unalienable Rights, that among these are Life, Liberty and the pursuit of happiness.***

PARAPHRASE: There are some truths so obvious that everyone should recognize their truth simply by thinking them through. This includes the truth that every person is as good as any other, and the truth that every person should be accorded the same basic rights. These rights include the right to not be hurt, harmed, or killed; the right to as much freedom (of thought, of movement, of choice of associates, of belief) as is possible; and the right to live their lives as they please.

---

***That to secure these rights, Governments are instituted among Men, deriving their just powers from the consent of the governed,***

PARAPHRASE: The main reason for having a government is to protect our rights to equality, life, liberty, and our own preferred way of living. Governments should have only the power we freely give it to protect our rights. Governments should not rule us; we should rule the government.

***That whenever any Form of Government becomes destructive of these ends, it is the Right of the People to alter or abolish it,***

PARAPHRASE: Whenever any government stops protecting our rights (to equality, life, liberty, and our own preferred way of living), we have a right to change that government or end it altogether. People have an inherent right to revolt against and overthrow any government that fails to enhance our quality of life, our equality, our freedom, and our preferred ways of living. If government is really doing its job, we should all of us experience maximum freedom in our lives and a minimum of restrictions. In a well-governed country, laws should be kept to an absolute minimum.

***and to institute new Government, laying its foundation on such principles and organizing its powers in such form, as to them shall seem most likely to effect their Safety and Happiness.***

PARAPHRASE: If we do overthrow a government that is failing to provide us with our natural rights, we should start a new government that does.

***Prudence, indeed, will dictate that Governments long established should not be changed for light and transient causes;***

PARAPHRASE: If we are practical, discreet, and have good judgment, we will not overthrow a government except for important and enduring reasons.

***and accordingly all experience hath shown that mankind are more disposed to suffer, while evils are sufferable, than to right themselves by abolishing the forms to which they are accustomed.***

PARAPHRASE: And, in fact, the whole of human history shows us that people are much more apt to suffer their rights being abused than to revolt against such abuse.

***But when a long train of abuses and usurpations, pursuing invariably the same Object evinces a design to reduce them under absolute Despotism, it is their right, it is their duty, to throw off such Government, and to provide new Guards for their future security.***

PARAPHRASE: When a government displays a long-standing disregard for the human rights of its own citizens, it is not only the right of such citizens, but also the obligation of such citizens, to revolt against the government and set up a new one that upholds its natural rights.

# The Declaration of Independence Specimen Answers—Form B

## Explicating the Thesis of a Text

### Statement of Thesis

All peoples in the world have a right to revolt against their government and establish a new government—if and when their human rights are systematically violated.

### Elaboration of Thesis

Periodically, people are governed in such a way as to oppress or exploit them and violate their rights as humans. When that occurs, the people so oppressed have a revolutionary right to set up their own country and government.

### Exemplification of Thesis

This situation occurred in France, leading to the French revolution; in America, leading to the American revolution; and in Russia, leading to the Russian revolution.

### Illustration of Thesis

A political revolution is like a divorce within a family, in which part of the family separates itself from another part and they go their separate ways. Each part becomes a family of its own, with a separate life. Divorces, like revolutions, usually occur when one or more persons have a long-standing grievance that they believe will never be redressed in the present family structure. Like political revolutions, divorces in the family sometimes involve violence.

# The Declaration of Independence Specimen Answers—Form C

## Explicating the Logic of a Text
## (An analysis of eight basic structures)

1. The authors' *purpose:* to enunciate human rights, and their violation, as a justification for the 1776 political revolt of American colonists against Great Britain.
2. The most important *questions,* problems, or issues in the text: Are there universal human rights? Under what conditions are people justified in attempting to overthrow a government? Were the colonists justified in their revolt against Great Britain?
3. The most significant *information* or data in the text: information supporting the view that American colonists were being denied basic rights, that they were suffering at the hands of the government.
4. The most basic *conclusions* of the author: that the proper function of governments is to protect the universal human rights of citizens so they can live the freest life possible; and that if a government fails to protect the human rights of its citizens, the people have the right to overthrow the government.
5. The most basic *concepts,* theories, or ideas used by the author: human rights, revolution, and the role and duty of government.
6. The most fundamental *assumptions* of the author: that all people have the same basic rights, that all governments have the same basic duties to the people, that governments should serve people rather than people serving governments.
7. The most significant *implications* of the text: that of people setting an example to the world by enunciating universal human rights, including, and most important, the right of revolution.
8. The author's *point of view:* seeing all humans as equal in worth and in human rights; at the same time, seeing all governments as having the obligation to be subservient to people, rather than to dominate them.

# The Declaration of Independence Specimen Answers—Form D

## Evaluating the Logic of a Text

1. **Do the authors say clearly what they mean, or is the text vague, confused, or muddled in some way?** The text is eminently clear, though written in the archaic language of the time.
2. Are the authors accurate in what they claim? The standard of accuracy applies most readily to the list of specific grievances that follows, but is not incorporated into the text here. The section of the declaration we read enunciates ideals, not facts. Most people in government would theoretically accept those ideals while violating them in practice. The UN Universal Declaration of Human Rights is a modern amplification of basic human rights. It has been signed by all of the nations in the world, yet the violation of human rights is a reality in virtually every country.
3. Are the authors sufficiently precise in providing details and specifics (when relevant)? Like the standard of accuracy, the standard of precision applies most readily to the list of specific grievances that follows the text we read here.
4. Are the authors true to their purpose or do they wander, thereby introducing irrelevant material? All of the text seems highly relevant to the central purpose of detailing human rights, and their violation, as a justification for the political revolt of American colonists against Great Britain.
5. Do the authors take us into the important complexities inherent in the subject, or is the writing superficial? In a very short text, the Declaration introduces concepts and ideals that are profoundly important in human life and history. Of course, there are many complexities inherent in the subject that are not discussed.
6. Do the authors consider other relevant points of view, or is the writing overly narrow in its perspective? As a political manifesto, it defends universal human rights and hence is broad in its sweep. At the same time, it excludes a "power rules in a hard, cruel, world" orientation, which seems to motivate many, if not most, politicians and seems to underlie most political reality.
7. Is the text internally consistent, or does it have contradictions? The text is highly consistent internally. At the same time it is arguably inconsistent with much U.S. foreign policy in the last hundred years or so.
8. Is what the text says significant, or is the subject dealt with in a trivial manner? This manifesto is one of the most significant documents in human history.
9. Does the author display fairness, or is the subject dealt with in an unfair manner? Because the Declaration of Independence defends the basic rights of all humans, it is, by implication, fair.

# On Civil Disobedience
# Specimen Answers—Form A
## Paraphrasing A Text Sentence by Sentence

***I heartily accept the motto, "That government is best which governs least"; and I should like to see it acted up to more rapidly and systematically.***

PARAPHRASE: The most effective form of government is one that establishes the least number of rules, regulations, and laws, so that people are as free as possible to make their own decisions and live in the ways they see fit. The U.S. government is not yet living up to this ideal and I, Thoreau, would like to see the government moving toward that ideal more quickly and more methodically.

---

***Carried out, it finally amounts to this, which also I believe, "That government is best which governs not at all";***

PARAPHRASE: The ideal form of government is one that places no rules and regulations on people whatsoever.

---

***and when men are prepared for it, that will be the kind of government which they will have.***

PARAPHRASE: When people can live rationally, respecting the rights and needs of others as a matter of course, making reasonable decisions in thinking through issues and problems, when they rise above needing to be restrained, they will then demand a government that doesn't interfere with their ability to live life as they so choose.

---

***Government is at best but an expedient; but most governments are usually, and all governments are sometimes, inexpedient.***

PARAPHRASE: Government, at best, is a necessary evil, a contrivance that is useful in the short run. But most governments typically are not useful and beneficial to people, and all governments sometimes fail to serve the people usefully.

---

***The objections which have been brought against a standing army, and they are many and weighty, and deserve to prevail, may also at last be brought against a standing government. The standing army is only an arm of the standing government. The government itself, which is only the mode which the people have chosen to execute their will, is equally liable to be abused and perverted before the people can act through it.***

PARAPHRASE: The problems inherent in established governments are similar to the problems that typically emerge where you have established armies within a country. And the two sets of problems are interrelated, because fixed armies are controlled by fixed governments. When governments are established, they presumably are established to carry out the desires of the people they represent. But they often become dysfunctional, failing to achieve their original purposes and intentions, and are used by the "powers that be" to serve the interests of those who are governing rather than those they should be representing. This often happens before the people even have the opportunity to take advantage of the expressed purposes and goals of the government. In other words, this problem seems to be almost a natural implication of an established government (given historical examples).

---

***Can there not be a government in which majorities do not virtually decide right and wrong, but conscience?...***

PARAPHRASE: Is it possible to be governed in such a way that one can decide for oneself what is right or wrong, based on one's own ethical sense of right and wrong, rather than having a government dictate what is right or wrong based on what most people think?

---

***Must the citizen ever for a moment, or in the least degree, resign his conscience to the legislator? Why has every man a conscience then? I think that we should be men first, and subjects afterward.***

PARAPHRASE: Individual citizens should never, under any circumstances or at any time, give up what they know to be ethically right and instead allow legislators to decide what is right. Why do people have the intellectual ability to figure out what is right and wrong if they are not willing to live in accordance with their sense of what is right? Doing what one deeply judges to be right takes precedence over doing what governments say we should or must do.

---

***It is not desirable to cultivate a respect for the law, so much as for the right. The only obligation which I have a right to assume is to do at any time what I think right....***

PARAPHRASE: It is much more important for people to develop a respect for and understanding of what is right than to uncritically adhere to laws (which may be unjust). The only thing that people are really obligated to do is what they think is right, not what the law says is right. (Of course, this assumes that people understand ethics, and can distinguish it from cultural norms and values.)

---

***If the injustice is part of the necessary friction of the machine of government, let it go, let it go;... If the injustice has a spring, or a pulley, or a rope, or a crank, exclusively for itself, then perhaps you can consider whether the remedy will not be worse than the evil;***

PARAPHRASE: Some situations and circumstances are inherently unjust to some people no matter what is done to reduce injustice within systems. It may be the case, for example, that reducing injustice leads to even greater injustice. If this is likely to happen, don't try to change the system. Let it keep functioning as it is.

---

***but if it is of such a nature that it requires you to be the agent of injustice to another, then, I say, break the law. Let your life be a counter friction to stop the machine.***

PARAPHRASE: But if the problems within the government are so great that by adhering to laws, you deny someone a fundamental human right, you are ethically obligated to break the law. In that case, stand up against the government. Do whatever you can to stop the government from unjust actions.

# *On Civil Disobedience*
# Specimen Answers—Form B
## Explicating the Thesis of a Text

### Statement of Thesis

All governments tend to abuse power, generate laws, and make decisions that unduly restrict people's freedom. Therefore, people are best served by governments that govern as little as possible. When people are able to live without being governed, they will demand to live without government. Moreover, people need to behave more in accordance with their conscience than in accordance with the law. If a law requires you to behave in an unjust way toward another, you are ethically obligated to break the law.

### Elaboration of Thesis

Though a democratic government is chosen by the people to carry out the will of the people, it is far too easy and common for governmental power to be used for purposes of vested interests rather than for the best interest of the people. When this happens, the rights of the people are subverted. Therefore a minimalist type of government is the best. But people can have such a government only when they think well enough to demand it and can live rationally without unnecessary governance. Some laws might be considered necessary evils, because to change such laws would lead only to greater injustices than the original law. But if the only way to change a truly unjust law is to refuse to abide by the law, a person of conscience will refuse. People should be willing to sacrifice themselves to reduce injustice caused by unfair laws.

### Exemplification of Thesis

For an example of a government making decisions that go against the will of the people, we might consider the U.S./Mexican War. Though the voters never approved of the war, it was nevertheless forced on the citizenry by politicians and business people who were greedy for more land, more power, and more profits. For an example of people breaking the law in the pursuit of justice, consider the issue of slavery in the U.S. in the 1800s. After slaves in the north were freed, many people helped slaves in the south escape to the north. Though they risked imprisonment for helping free slaves on southern plantations (and, in essence breaking the law), many people were willing to do this rather than abide by an unjust law.

### Illustration of Thesis

Governments abusing power and doing what is in their interest rather than the interest of the people is similar to bureaucrats designing regulations to fit their own desires or the desires of pressure groups rather than the needs of the people the bureaucracy is supposed to serve.

To illustrate the idea of acting against the law to bring about change, consider children's peer groups and how they tend to act toward "outsiders." Often a peer group expects everyone in the group to accept and go along with an unjust act. For example, it is common for bullying to be practiced toward outsiders of children's peer groups. Bullying, then, is the accepted practice. Those in the group who object to bullying are usually subjected to penalties from the group—for example, they may be ridiculed or kicked out of the group. When children in such a group decide to go against the group, their defiance is similar to the kind of ethical behavior Thoreau is calling for. They are rebelling against the authority of the peer group, even if it means they will suffer as a result.

# *On Civil Disobedience*
# Specimen Answers—Form C
## Explicating the Logic of a Text
### (An analysis of eight basic structures)

### Purpose

The purpose of this excerpt is to convince the reader that governments should serve the people and that the people need to hold the government accountable for doing so, even if this means that the people have to break the law to bring about justice.

### Key Questions

1. What is the primary responsibility of government?
2. How do governments tend to function, with respect to its people?
3. How are people obligated to behave toward the government?
4. How are governments obligated to behave toward the people?
5. Is it possible to have a government wherein conscience is the guiding concept instead of vested interest?
6. How can the people best hold the government accountable to the people?

### Information

The information used in the author's reasoning is not stated but implied (and may be stated in the chapter from which this excerpt was taken). To examine the information the author uses to support his arguments, one would need to analyze the information provided by the author. If no information is provided by the author, one would need to identify examples of government behavior in general to see if this is a well-reasoned argument (looking specifically for ethical or unethical behavior, justice or injustice caused by the government). To determine the extent to which a *particular government* functions ethically or unethically, one would need to examine cases of government decisions and actions, as well as its laws, policies, and procedures, and the ethical implications of its actions.

Information about the problems inherent in standing armies is also being used in this argument (information that the reader should presumably already know, or will be given in the full text).

### Inferences (Conclusions)

1. The best government is the government that grants the greatest number of liberties and rights for its people.
2. Ideally, there would be no government—and this is what people will have when they think well enough to eliminate government.

3. Most governments typically are not useful and beneficial to people, and all governments sometimes fail to serve the people.
4. People within the government are likely to abuse their power before the people even benefit from the government they put into power (in other words, the abuses by the government begin almost immediately upon establishment of the government).
5. When abiding by the law results in greater injustice than refusing to do so, people have an ethical obligation to break the law.
6. The main obligation that people have is to do what is ethically right in any given situation.
7. If there is any way to work within the law to bring about justice and avoid injustices that would result from eliminating the law, then people should work within the law.

## Concepts

The key concept in this excerpt is *civil disobedience,* defined as the ethical obligation to go against the law when the law causes greater injustices than it rectifies. Other key concepts include: *ethical obligation* (equate with conscience), *government* ("the mode which the people have chosen to execute their will"), the distinction between behaving in accordance with the law versus behaving in accordance with what is right (*ethics* versus the *law*).

## Assumptions

1. If enough people break the law to stop injustice, the government will be forced to reconsider and reformulate the law.
2. People who understand ethics and behave in accordance with what is ethically right in a situation do not need to be governed (and have a right not to be governed).
3. At this time in history (the time that this excerpt was written), people did not fully understand ethics, which is why they needed a government.
4. People are theoretically capable of understanding ethics and living ethical lives.
5. Any and all forms of government are inherently unethical to some extent.
6. People who read these excerpts will already have some background knowledge of the problems inherent in standing armies (and can apply that knowledge to understand the problems in government).
7. People have a "right" to do what they think is ethically right in a situation.
8. People should be willing to make sacrifices to bring about justice for others (and they are ethically responsible to do so).
9. People will eventually be so adept at ethical reasoning that they will not need to be governed.

## Implications

If people accept this line of reasoning, either partially or completely, the following implications are likely:

1. People will conceptualize government very differently than most people now conceptualize it—with a responsibility to serve the people, to serve the needs and desires of the people above any other goal.
2. People will take more responsibility for analyzing and assessing laws to see if they result in just (or unjust) treatment for people.
3. When people identify unjust laws, or laws that lead to injustice, they may challenge the law, or refuse to abide by the law.
4. People will not assume that the government is concerned with their best interest.

If people reject this line of reasoning, they will likely fail to gain insight into the most common problems in government and its common abuses.

## Point of View

It consists in looking at governments as ethically responsible for serving the good of the people, but often causing injustices (either implicitly or explicitly).

It consists in seeing people as responsible for challenging unjust laws.

# On Civil Disobedience
# Specimen Answers—Form D
## Evaluating the Logic of a Text

1. **Do the authors say clearly what they mean, or is the text vague, confused, or muddled in some way?** The text is clear. We understand from the text precisely what the author means.
2. Is the author accurate in what he claims? The standard of accuracy applies most readily to the examples Thoreau provides to support his conclusions that governments often act in opposition to the needs and desires of the people. These examples are included in the larger text from which this text was excerpted. However, since any informed person could easily list a number of examples in support of Thoreau's claims, his main conclusions appear to be accurate.
3. Is the author sufficiently precise in providing details and specifics (when relevant)? Like the standard of accuracy, the standard of precision applies most readily to the list of examples supporting Thoreau's claims that governments often function unethically.
4. Is the author true to his purpose or does he wander, thereby introducing irrelevant material? All of the text seems highly relevant to the central purpose of persuading people to see that governments are obligated to serve the people and that people are obligated to hold the government accountable for unethical actions.
5. Does the author take us into the important complexities inherent in the subject, or is the writing superficial? In this very short text, the author does a good job of helping readers begin to see the problems inherent in most governing bodies and the laws created by governments. Yet, we would need to read further in the text to see how Thoreau recommends that people "break the law," that is, how realistic and feasible it would be for people to actually break the law to bring about change in the justice system. We would have to think through whether and to what extent breaking the law will actually lead to change, and whether it is reasonable to ask people to break the law, especially when the punishment would likely be harsh (especially in a country like the U.S. where punishments often far exceed what is reasonable given the "crime" they commit).
6. Does the author consider other relevant points of view, or is the writing overly narrow in its perspective? As a political directive, Thoreau's position is broad in scope. He is clearly concerned with creating a more just society, as he calls on his readers to do what they can to reduce the amount of injustice within their own culture. He is concerned about the rights and needs of all people within a society, which is clear evidence of a broad perspective.

7. Is the text internally consistent, or does it have contradictions? The two main points Thoreau makes—that governments tend to be unethical by their very nature, and that people have a responsibility to do what they can to force their government to act ethically—are consistent with one another.
8. Is what the text says significant, or is the subject dealt with in a trivial manner? This text is considered one of the most significant documents in human history. The subject of injustice at the hands of the government is significant. Moreover, Thoreau treats the subject with a high level of gravity—especially in calling on people to break the law to bring about greater justice. In fact, very few people are willing to break any laws to bring about greater justice to those caught in an unjust system. Unlike Thoreau, people tend to think about this subject either (1) not at all, or (2) in a superficial, non-courageous way.
9. Does the author display fairness, or is the subject dealt with in an unfair manner? Because the text defends the basic rights of all humans, it is, by implication, fair. The concept of fairness and justice lie at the very heart of Thoreau's argument.

# *The Art of Loving*
# Specimen Answers—Form A
## Paraphrasing a Text Sentence by Sentence

*Is love an art? Then it requires knowledge and effort.*

PARAPHRASE: If love is an art, involving skills and abilities, it requires deep understanding and the motivation to apply that understanding.

---

***Or is love a pleasant sensation, which to experience is a matter of chance, something one "falls into" if one is lucky?***

PARAPHRASE: Or perhaps love is strictly an enjoyable physical feeling, not something requiring skill, but rather an accidental occurrence or coincidence that just happens to people.

---

***This little book is based on the former premise, while undoubtedly the majority of people today believe in the latter.***

*The Art of Loving,* Not that people think that love is not important. They are starved for it; they watch endless numbers of films about happy and unhappy love stories, they listen to hundreds of trashy songs about love—yet hardly anyone thinks that there is anything that needs to be learned about love.

PARAPHRASE: Most people value love, at least at some level. In fact, they crave it. We know this because they watch innumerable movies about love and listen to endless vulgar songs about love. Yet, almost no one thinks that the ability to love is something that must be learned.

---

***This peculiar attitude is based on several premises which either singly or combined tend to uphold it. Most people see the problem of love primarily as that of being loved, rather than that of loving, of one's capacity to love. Hence the problem to them is how to be loved, how to be lovable.***

PARAPHRASE: This dysfunctional way in which people tend to think of love is based on one or more beliefs they hold about love. People primarily see the difficulty of love as trying to figure out how to get love from someone else rather than giving love to someone else. They therefore focus their energy on getting others to love them. They try to appear engaging, charming, or adorable to attract a lover.

---

***In pursuit of this aim they follow several paths. One, which is especially used by men, is to be successful, to be as powerful and rich as the social margin of one's position permits. Another, used especially by women, is to make oneself attractive, by cultivating one's body, dress, etc.***

PARAPHRASE: To achieve the goal of "being lovable," men tend to use a different strategy than women use. Men strive to achieve a position of status, which usually involves having as much power and money as they can. Women tend to emphasize making themselves physically attractive to the opposite sex, through adorning their body, attending to their clothing, and the like.

***Other ways of making oneself attractive, used both by men and women, are to develop pleasant manners, interesting conversation, to be helpful, modest, inoffensive. Many of the ways to make oneself lovable are the same as those used to make oneself successful, "to win friends and influence people." As a matter of fact, what most people in our culture mean by being lovable is essentially a mixture between being popular and having sex appeal.***

PARAPHRASE: Both men and women strive for appealing manners and a conversational style that renders them attractive, and therefore "lovable" to the opposite sex. They try to appear cooperative, supportive, unassuming, and unobjectionable. These same strategies are used to appear successful in others' eyes, to gain friends and win over people. To most people, being lovable is really the same as being sexy and well liked.

---

***The active character of [genuine] love becomes evident in the fact that it always implies certain basic elements, common to all forms of love. These are care, responsibility, respect, and knowledge.... Love is the active concern for the life and the growth of that which we love....***

PARAPHRASE: Certain basic components of love exist within any form of real love. These are thoughtfulness, dependability, consideration, and understanding. When we love someone, we seek their best welfare. We show our concern for what happens to them.

---

***Respect is the ability to see a person as he is, to be aware of his unique individuality. Respect means the concern that the other person should grow and unfold as he is. Respect, thus, implies the absence of exploitation. I want the loved person to grow and unfold for his own sake, and in his own ways, and not for the purpose of serving me. If I love the other person, I feel one with him or her, but with him as he is, not as I need him to be as an object for my use.***

PARAPHRASE: When we respect others, we don't need to idealize them. We can see them as they really are, as persons with distinctive characteristics. We want them to develop as they want to develop and be what they want to be. We do not treat them as objects to be used for our own selfish interests. When we love others, we feel deeply connected to them as they are, with all their unique qualities.

---

***It is clear that respect is possible only if I have achieved independence; if I can stand and walk without needing crutches, without having to dominate and exploit anyone else. Respect exists only on the basis of freedom "l'amour est l'enfant de la liberté" as an old French song says; love is the child of freedom, never of domination.***

PARAPHRASE: I can respect another only if I am myself an autonomous person, if I can stand on my own two feet, without the need to lean on others for support, without the need to use others, to control them so that they might serve me. Respect can happen only when people are allowed to be what they want to be, never when they are being forced to live a certain way against their will.

---

***To love somebody is not just a strong feeling—it is a decision, it is a judgment, it is a promise.***

PARAPHRASE: Love is not just a feeling. It is a choice, a resolution, a commitment, a pledge.

# *The Art of Loving*
# Specimen Answers—Form B
## Explicating the Thesis of a Text

### Statement of Thesis
Loving another person is an art. It requires knowledge, skill, and insight. Genuine love doesn't just happen to people. It must be cultivated through deep commitment. This way of looking at love is very different from the way most people do.

### Elaboration of Thesis
We need to change the way we think about love. We should abandon images that imply that love is mysterious and beyond our control. We should see it as a form of strength in which we give to others what enhances their well-being. When we are weak, we want others to hold us up, to protect us, to take care of us. Weakness is not a sound basis for giving love. When we truly love others, we want them to develop and grow. We do not use them to serve us.

### Exemplification of Thesis
In many Hollywood films and soap operas, love is associated with passionate, out-of-control accusations and cruel acts, often followed by apologies and sexual intimacy. Jealousy, envy, and an attempt to control the other are all commonplace in the public image of lovers in action. Genuine love, as a long-term commitment to the well-being of others, does not make for action-packed drama. Portrayals of genuine love are rarely depicted in Hollywood films.

### Illustration of Thesis
Defective forms of love are like a suffocating vine that attaches itself to a plant and eventually kills it. The vine dominates the plant, requiring the plant to submit to its domination. But genuine love neither dominates nor submits. Genuine love can exist only between relative equals, like two plants growing side by side, sharing the same sunlight and soil nutrients, allowing one another the space to grow as unique individuals.

# *The Art of Loving*
# Specimen Answers—Form C

## Explicating the Logic of a Text
### (An analysis of eight basic structures)

### Purpose

The purpose of the text is to explore the meaning of "love," to connect it with other related concepts, such as care, responsibility, respect, and knowledge; and to convince the reader that the concept of "love," at its very root, has a deep meaning, requiring deep commitment and responsibility (rather than being treated superficially, as is common in society).

### Key Questions

The main questions that this text addresses are: What is love? What does it require of a person? How do most people think of love?

### Information

The key information in this text are the examples given that describe the way most people think of love, information such as:

1. People "watch endless numbers of films about happy and unhappy love stories."
2. They "listen to hundreds of trashy songs about love."
3. Men, especially, try to appear "as powerful and rich as the social margin of one's position permits."
4. Women, especially, try to "make oneself attractive by cultivating one's body, dress, etc."
5. Both men and women try to make themselves attractive by developing "pleasant manners, interesting conversations," by being "helpful, modest, inoffensive."

### Key Conclusions

There are several main conclusions in this text, including:

1. Love is an "art," requiring commitment and deep concern for the well-being of those whom one loves. It is not just a strong feeling, but "a decision, it is a judgment, it is a promise."
2. Most people in our culture have a distorted view of love. They consider "being lovable [to be] essentially a mixture between being popular and having sex appeal."
3. When you love someone, you "want the loved person to grow and unfold for his own sake, and in his own ways, and not for the purpose of serving [you]."

## Key Concepts

The main concept in this text is the concept of love, which, according to Fromm, requires, "care, responsibility, respect, and knowledge...the active concern for the life and the growth of that which we love...to love...is a decision, it is a judgment, it is a promise."

## Assumptions

Here are some of the beliefs Fromm takes for granted in writing this text:

1. Very few people understand love at a deep level. They have never taken the concept of love seriously.
2. You can't truly love someone unless you understand the concept of love.
3. Humans naturally seek loving relationships, but because society has created a dysfunctional concept of love, most people will never truly love, nor truly be loved.
4. People generally think of love as something that is done to them by another person–when someone serves their needs and desires.
5. To understand any deep concept well, one must analyze the concept at a deep level, and apply the concept to many potential cases (as Fromm has done with the concept of love).
6. Most people are unhappy in the relationships they define as loving because those relationships are usually empty, disappointing, superficial.
7. You cannot love someone if you do not know that person at a deep level.

## Implications

If people take this line of reasoning seriously, they will reconsider the way they view love. They will recognize the superficial nature of the concept of love generally used in our culture. They may look at their own "loving" relationships and assess the extent to which their relationships fit Fromm's definition of love, or whether their relationships are superficial, distorted, or dysfunctional. They will begin to see love as something requiring deep commitment and respect, responsibility and caring. Their loving relationships will tend to be far more rewarding and healthy.

If people fail to take this line of reasoning seriously, they will most likely use a dysfunctional, superficial concept of love as they develop relationships with significant others. They may go the whole of their lives in such a relationship. Their "loving" relationships will most likely be unsatisfactory, likely leading to negative consequences and/or a pervasive feeling of frustration or negativity. They will seek "love" through superficial means, rather than deep understandings.

## Point of View

The author is looking at *love,* and seeing it as deep idea, as a process requiring respect, caring, responsibility, and knowledge, as something that you have to work at diligently and consistently. The author also looks at people in our culture as having a distorted, dysfunctional, and superficial view of love, a view that leads to unhappiness and a lack of deep fulfillment.

# *The Art of Loving*
# Specimen Answers—Form D
## Evaluating the Logic of a Text

1. **Do the authors say clearly what they mean, or is the text vague, confused, or muddled in some way?** The text is clear. We understand from the text what the author means.
2. **Is the author accurate in what he claims?** The author provides a number of intuitive examples to support his conclusion that people often have a superficial, dysfunctional concept of love. Given what can easily be seen in everyday life, these examples appear quite reasonable.
3. Is the author sufficiently precise in providing details and specifics (when relevant)? Yes, Fromm provides enough detail in his examples and reasoning to make clear the view he is defending.
4. Is the author true to his purpose or does he wander, thereby introducing irrelevant material? All of the text seems highly relevant to the central purpose of helping people understand a deep and significant concept of love.
5. Does the author take us into the important complexities inherent in the subject, or is the writing superficial? The concept of love detailed by Fromm is profound. In fact one of his main arguments is that we must think deeply to understand the nature of genuine love. By using pertinent and intuitive examples, the author helps the reader begin to understand the complexities of love, and the importance of getting beyond a superficial understanding of it.
6. Does the author consider other relevant points of view, or is the writing overly narrow in its perspective? Fromm is concerned to contrast the everyday view of love with one that goes beneath the surface and makes clear what we imply when we say to someone that we really love him or her. Fromm is not trying to consider and analyze other possible conflicting points of view concerning love. Given his purpose, he is not reasoning in a narrow way.
7. Is the text internally consistent, or does it have contradictions? In so far as we can see from this brief text, there are no contradictions in Fromm's concept of love. The ingredients that he sees as essential to the concept of love – care, respect, responsibility and knowledge – are interrelated, and, in this passage, he begins to detail their interrelationships.

3. Is what the text says significant, or is the subject dealt with in a trivial manner? This excerpt is taken from the book, The Art Of Loving. This book, written a half a century ago, is still considered one of the most significant and authoritative texts on the concept of love. Again, the author is attempting to convince the reader that

the concept of love is by its very nature deep, not trivial; and to treat it trivially is to cause numerous problems in human relationships.

4. Does the author display fairness, or is the subject dealt with in an unfair manner? Fromm has a well-defined and limited objective---to contrast our everyday behavior in what we unreflectively think are loving relationships with the ideal implicit in the way we talk about love. For Fromm, this "ideal" implies that love is an art. His goal is not to consider other ways to view love. Thus, "fairness" (to other points of view) does not seem relevant. If asked, Fromm would probably admit that he has not provided a range of different possible points of view concerning love. On the other hand, those who hold a different view of love would doubtless argue that he should have considered alternative conceptions of love.

# The Logic of Ecology
# Specimen Answers—Form CC

## Explicating the Logic of a Subject or Discipline
### as Detailed in a Textbook

A careful third level reading of a well-written ecology textbook should disclose essentially the following logic:

**Goals of Ecologists.** Ecologists seek to understand plants and animals as they exist in nature, with emphasis on their interrelationships, interdependence, and interactions with the environment. They work to understand all the influences that combine to produce and modify an animal or given plant, and thus to account for its existence and peculiarities within its habitat.

Questions Ecologists Ask. How do plants and animals interact? How do animals interact with each other? How to plants and animals depend on one another? How do the varying ecosystems function within themselves? How do they interact with other ecosystems? How are plants and animals affected by environmental influences? How do animals and plants grow, develop, die, and replace themselves? How do plants and animals create balances between each other? What happens when plants and animals become unbalanced?

**Information Ecologists Use.** The primary information used by ecologists is gained through observing plants and animals themselves, their interactions, and how they live within their environments. Ecologists note how animals and plants are born, how they reproduce, how they die, how they evolve, how they are affected by environmental changes. They also use information from other disciplines including chemistry, meteorology, and geology.

Judgments Ecologists Make. Ecologists make judgments about how ecosystems naturally function, about how animals and plants within them function, about why they function as they do. They make judgments about how ecosystems become out of balance and what can be done to bring them back into balance. They make judgments about how natural communities should be grouped and classified.

**Concepts that Guide Ecologists' Thinking.** One of the most fundamental concepts in ecology is "ecosystem." Ecosystem is defined as a group of living things, dependent on one another and living in a particular habitat. Ecologists study how differing ecosystems function. Another key concept in ecology is "ecological succession," the natural pattern of change occurring within every ecosystem when natural processes are undisturbed. This pattern includes the birth, development, death, and then replacement of natural communities. Ecologists have grouped communities into larger units called "biomes." These are regions throughout the world classified according to physical features, including temperature, rainfall, and type of vegetation. Another fundamental concept in geology is "balance of nature," the natural process of birth, reproduction, eating and being eaten, which keeps animal/plant communities fairly stable. Other key concepts include imbalances, energy, nutrients, population growth, diversity, habitat, competition, predation, parasitism, adaptation, co-evolution, succession and climax communities, and conservation.

Key Assumptions Ecologists Make. Ecologists assume that patterns exist within animal/plant communities; that these communities should be studied and classified; that animals and plants often depend on one another and modify one another; that balances must be maintained within ecosystems.

Implications of Ecology. The study of ecology leads to numerous implications for life on earth. By studying balance of nature, for example, we can see when nature is out of balance, as in the current "population explosion," and begin to reverse the population problem. We can see how pesticides, designed to kill pests on farm crops, also lead to the harm of mammals and birds, either directly or indirectly through food webs. We can also learn how over-farming causes erosion and depletion of soil nutrients.

The Point of View of Ecologists. Ecologists look at plants and animals and see them functioning in relationship with one another within their habitats, and needing to be in balance for the earth to be healthy and sustainable.

# The Logic of Economics
# Specimen Answers—Form CC

## Explicating the Logic of a Subject or Discipline
### as Detailed in a Textbook

A careful third level reading of a well-written economics textbook should disclose essentially the following logic:

Goals of Economists. To develop theories that explain the distribution of goods and services within a society, as well as theories that define how goods and services should be distributed.

Questions Economists Ask. How are goods and services produced, distributed, and consumed within any given society? How should they be? What is the best way to determine what people should get and how, on the one hand, they should be allowed to get it (e.g., to what extent should people be encouraged to pursue wealth and power principally for their own benefit)? On the other hand, to what extent should society try to provide equal access to education, wealth, and power? What are the strengths and weaknesses of competing economic theories?

Information Economists Use. Economists from differing schools of thought disagree on the information they use in reasoning through economic problems. Those who favor capitalism, for example, focus on information about supply of products versus demand, consumer preferences, consumer spending, business investments, and government support of business. In solving economic problems, they emphasize information about how to keep aggregate demand high. Those who favor socialism focus on information that reveals the impact of the distribution of wealth on the well-being of everyone, especially the poor and disadvantaged. Their ideal is to distribute wealth so that resources are made available as equally as possible, taking into account the crucial problem of how to motivate people to contribute to the well-being of others as well as themselves. The information that economists use is ultimately determined by the way they conceptualize ideal economic systems and the questions implied by the economic theories that guide their thinking.

Judgments Economists Make. Economists make judgments about how best to stabilize and enhance the distribution, production, and use of goods and services. They make these judgments in accordance with their economic philosophies, considering trends and patterns of individual business and government spending, economic health, and distribution of wealth.

Concepts that Guide Economists' Thinking. Economics is the study of how goods, services, and resources are/should be distributed and used within human societies. Leading economic concepts have evolved, especially through the last 200 years. Some of them are: the principle of competition, law of supply and demand, utilitarianism, capitalism, socialism, communism, Marxism, exploitation, class conflict between economic strata (especially between workers and employers), private property, free markets, self-interest, psychological variables influencing economic behavior, assumption of scarcity, law of diminishing returns, principles of marginal utility and productivity, aggregate demand, labor theory of value, Malthusian population doctrine, and Keynesian economics.

Key Assumptions Economists Make. By studying the ways and means for distributing goods and services, economic systems can become more stable and more fair to the people who vie for resources within those systems. Beyond this shared assumption, economists' assumptions differ according to their philosophies, values, and theories. Those who favor capitalism assume that humans are fundamentally selfish and that only a system that utilizes the driving force of human selfishness will be realistic. Socialists, in contrast, assume that education can be used to shift the emphasis in human activity from self-aggrandizement to altruism.

Implications of Economy. The implications that economic theories generate vary from theory to theory. Which of the theoretical implications become actual consequences are a matter of continual debate. The debate focuses on what actual consequences seem to be accounted for by this or that economic theory and what consequences (good or bad) result from variables other than those postulated by a given theory. For example, did the Great Depression of the 1930s result from a deep flaw in capitalist theory, or did it result from a failure to practice the theory thoroughly enough?

The Point of View of Economists. Economists look at the distribution of goods and services within a society, along with the distribution of power that distribution entails, as a crucial object of systematic study.

# Appendix A

## The Logic of an Excerpt, Article, Essay, or Chapter

One important way to understand an excerpt, essay, article or chapter is through the analysis of the parts of the author's reasoning. Once you have done this, you can evaluate the author's reasoning using intellectual standards. Here is a template to follow:

1. The main **purpose** of this article is _____. (Here you are trying to state, as accurately as possible, the author's intent in writing the article. What was the author trying to accomplish?)
2. The key **question** that the author is addressing is _____. (Your goal is to figure out the key question that was in the mind of the author when he/she wrote the article. What was the key question addressed in the article?)
3. The most important **information** in this article is _____. (You want to identify the key information the author used, or presupposed, in the article to support his/her main arguments. Here you are looking for facts, experiences, and/or data the author is using to support his/her conclusions.)
4. The main **inferences** in this article are _____. (You want to identify the most important conclusions the author comes to and presents in the article.)
5. The key **concept(s)** we need to understand in this article is (are) _____. By these concepts the author means _____. (To identify these ideas, ask yourself: What are the most important ideas that you would have to know to understand the author's line of reasoning? Then briefly elaborate what the author means by these ideas.)
6. The main **assumption(s)** underlying the author's thinking is are) _____. (Ask yourself: What is the author taking for granted [that might be questioned]? The assumptions are generalizations that the author does not think he/she has to defend in the context of writing the article, and they are usually unstated. This is where the author's thinking logically begins.)

7a. If we take this line of reasoning seriously, the **implications** are _____. (What consequences are likely to follow if people take the author's line of reasoning seriously? Here you are to pursue the logical implications of the author's position. You should include implications that the author states, and also those that the author does not state.)

7b. If we fail to take this line of reasoning seriously, the **implications** are _____. (What consequences are likely to follow if people ignore the author's reasoning?)

8. The main **point(s) of view** presented in this article is (are) _____. (The main question you are trying to answer here is: What is the author looking at, and how is he/she seeing it? For example, in this mini-guide we are looking at "analysis" and seeing it "as requiring one to understand" and routinely apply the elements of reasoning when thinking through problems, issues, subjects, and so forth.)

If you truly understand these structures as they interrelate in an excerpt, article, essay, or chapter, you should be able to empathically role-play the thinking of the author. These are the eight basic structures that define all reasoning. They are the essential elements of thought.

# The Thinker's Guide Library

Rowman & Littlefield is the proud distributor of the Thinker's Guide Library developed by the Foundation for Critical Thinking. Please visit www.rowman.com or call 1-800-462-640 for more information. Bulk order discounts available.

## For Everyone

**The Miniature Guide to Critical Thinking Concepts & Tools, Eighth Edition**
Paperback 9781538134948
eBook 9781538134955

**The Thinker's Guide to Ethical Reasoning**
Paperback 9780944583173
eBook 9781538133781

**The Thinker's Guide to Fallacies**
Paperback 9780944583272
eBook 9781538133774

**The Art of Asking Essential Questions**
Paperback 9780944583166
eBook 9781538133804

**The Thinker's Guide for Conscientious Citizens on How to Detect Media Bias and Propaganda in National and World News, Fourth Edition**
Paperback 9780944583203
eBook 9781538133897

**The Thinker's Guide to Engineering Reasoning**
Paperback 9780944583333
eBook 9781538133798

**The Thinker's Guide to Analytic Thinking**
Paperback 9780944583197
eBook 9781538133750

**The Thinker's Guide to Socratic Questioning**
Paperback 9780944583319
eBook 9781538133842

**The Nature and Functions of Critical & Creative Thinking**
Paperback 9780944583265
eBook 9781538133958

**Thinker's Guide to the Human Mind**
Paperback 9780944583586
eBook 9781538133880

**The Thinker's Guide to Scientific Thinking**
Paperback 9780985754426
eBook 9781538133811

**The Thinker's Guide to Clinical Reasoning**
Paperback 9780944583425
eBook 9781538133873

## For Students

**The Aspiring Thinker's Guide to Critical Thinking**
Paperback 9780944583418
eBook 9781538133767

**The Thinker's Guide for Students on How to Study & Learn a Discipline, Second Edition**
Paperback 9781632340009
eBook 9781538133835

**The International Critical Thinking Reading and Writing Test, Second Edition**
Paperback 9780944583326
eBook 9781538133965

**The Student Guide to Historical Thinking**
Paperback 9780944583463
eBook 9781538133941

**How to Read a Paragraph, second edition**
Paperback 9780944583494
eBook 9781538133828

**How to Write a Paragraph**
Paperback 9780944583227
eBook 9781538133866

## For Educators

**The Miniature Guide to Practical Ways for Promoting Active and Cooperative Learning, Third Edition**
Paperback 9780944583135
eBook 9781538133903

**A Critical Thinker's Guide to Educational Fads**
Paperback 9780944583340
eBook 9781538133910

**A Guide for Educators to Critical Thinking Competency Standards**
Paperback 9780944583302
eBook 9781538133934

**How to Improve Student Learning: 30 Practical Ideas**
Paperback 9780944583555
eBook 9781538133859

**The Thinker's Guide to Intellectual Standards**
Paperback 9780944583395
eBook 9781538133927